Loving
MYSELF

RENEE' HALL

Editing:
PeriSean B. Hall
The Word Doctor

Proofreading:
Lisa Darling
Katrina Gibson

Interior & Cover Layout & Design:
Tarsha L. Campbell

Published by:
DOMINIONHOUSE
Publishing & Design, LLC
P.O. Box 681938 | Orlando, Florida 32868 | 407.703.4800
www.mydominionhouse.com
*The Lord gave the word: great was the company of those
that published it. (Psalms 68:11)*

Loving Myself

When I don't love myself, I will settle for less
When I don't love myself,
I will think I don't deserve the best
When I don't love myself,
I will hide behind sin and shame
When I don't love myself, I will put others to blame

But when I love myself, I won't settle for less
And when I love myself, I will think I deserve the best
When I love myself,
I won't hide behind sin and shame
When I love myself, I won't put others to blame

Because I love myself, I will stand strong and fight
Because I love myself, I will fight with all my might
Because I love myself, I will open my eyes and see
Because I love myself, and see that Jesus lives in me

ACKNOWLEDGEMENTS

I would love to first acknowledge God for making it possible to be at this place in my life. For I know without Him everything I'm doing during this season would not be possible.

Secondly, I would like to acknowledge my mother, Verna Fields. Mom you are the best. Thank you mom for being a real good mother to your kids. I know that it was difficult raising four children alone as a single parent but God saw us through.

To my sisters, Lisa and Allison Huewitt, thank you for listening to me preach and sing to ya'll all the time. I love you both so much.

Special thanks to Plarious Hall, my adorable husband of 25 years. You always supported me while I stayed up late gathering notes together, writing poems, and creating new ideas. You are the best.

To my awesome daughter, Akilah Hall, thank you for always being there to help me email letters, retype papers, and give advice on some of the decisions that I had to make concerning my projects.

I would like to thank God for blessing me with my two grandkids, (Christian and Kennedi Hall) that inspire me to be the best that I can be. Gammie loves you very much.

To Bishop and First Lady Dennison of Compassionate Outreach Ministries, thank you for being my spiritual parents and teaching me the way of holiness and excellence. Thank you for all the amazing marriage retreats, women conferences, revivals, and awesome Sunday services. I truly have had an Eph. 3:20 experience for the last five magnificent years.

Thank you to Deacon Leon Rowe, and his lovely wife Diane Rowe, for being godly mentors that truly represent love, godliness and holiness.

And to all my brothers and sisters in Christ at Compassionate Outreach Ministries, I truly love you all.

To my wife, Cathryn, who keeps me centered and helps me deal with the realities of life.

TABLE OF CONTENTS

This book has been years in the making. The Lord has given me so much information over a course of time as he first began to lead me on my journey towards completing this book. I know it will be a blessing to many because so many women, men, and children have not learned how to love themselves.

The key to learning to love yourself is having an understanding of God's unconditional love towards you. When you don't understand the unconditional love of God you will be ill prepared to love yourself properly as He intends for you to. You see, God looks past your faults and sees your needs. He knows you have shortcomings and are human (flesh) with undeniable flaws. These flaws can be a result of your painful past. If you think about it, many of us came from dysfunctional families. If you didn't then you are one of the lucky ones, but most of us did.

There were families that did not have a father figure that established a healthy atmosphere, structured and having boundaries that could mold the family into a successful household. There were also single parent homes that did not have enough money for the house to run to its full capacity. And in some homes, physical, sexual, and mental abuse was commonplace. Within the context of all these different experiences it caused a misrepresentation of love. As this misrepresentation of love plagued many of us, it then permeated into our communities, and then it flowed to our society, and on into the World at large. But once you experience the true love of God, it changes your perspective, releasing new understanding and insight in your life.

God sent His Son to die on the cross for our sin, so that you can have a new opportunity to live again. What do I mean by live again? By the works of Jesus Christ dying, you get a chance to understand and apply the love of God to your life. This is why I wrote this book, which was inspired by a poem I wrote called "Loving Myself". The poem has twelve verses that I separated by verse and expounded on it as the Holy Spirit gave me revelation. The Holy Spirit taught me that there is a process that each born again Christian must go through to truly love themselves. The process consist of three levels we have to experience to reach spiritual maturity in our love walk in order to live the victorious life that God has ordained through His love and His dear Son, Jesus Christ.

As a child of God you must transition from one level to the next as you grow spiritually. In this book, as I expound upon each verse of the "Loving Myself" poem, you will find that spiritual maturity will take place as you continue in prayer, praise, worship, trust, believing, obeying, and honoring God with your whole heart. Upon completion of this book you will gain revelation and strength to stand strong in God. Your spiritual eyes will also be opened so you can see that greater is He that's in you than He that is in the World, because it is Jesus that lives on the inside of you. I pray that you enjoy the poem and the life changing principles in this book. Allow what you receive to empower you and transform you into a mature Christian that lives your life from a position of power and authority through love.

******

Love Fact:

There are multiple testimonies of men, women, boys, and girls that have experienced the unconditional love of God and have testified that His love has taught them how to love themselves.

Three Levels to Spiritual Maturity
(Loving Myself)

First level: When I don't love myself:
1. Settle for less
2. I don't think I deserve the best
3. Hide behind sin and shame
4. Putting others to blame

Second level: But when I love myself:
1. Won't settle for less
2. I will think I deserve the best
3. Won't hide behind sin and shame
4. Won't put others to blame

Third level: Because I love myself:
1. I will stand strong and fight
2. I will fight with all of my might
3. Open up my eyes and see
4. See that Jesus lives in me

These are the three levels that were revealed to me by the Holy Spirit that one must go through to reach spiritual maturity.

"God really does love you, yes, I am talking about you!! There you have it, so what are you going to do about it? This revelation about love has come to you to give you light and a chance to walk in a whole new direction."

Chapter 1

WHEN I DON'T LOVE MYSELF

I find it amazing that there are countless numbers of people that are not rehearsing what I am writing about in this book. Many people are not loving themselves because they are too busy abusing themselves by various means. They don't count themselves worthy of the abundant love that only God can give. They have no hope, or they have no idea that there is hope. They abuse themselves with alcohol, sex, drugs, over eating, gambling, lying, cheating, stealing and the list goes on and on. I have found that the opposite of love is hate; but we won't dare say that these people hate themselves. Hate is a strong word and it may sound like some people really do not care about themselves, but the truth of the matter is they might care but they may lack information on how to love themselves properly.

If this sounds like you then I want to tell you a secret, are you ready? God really does love you, yes, I am talking about you!! There you have it, so what are you going to do about it? This revelation about love has come to you to give you light and a chance to walk in a whole new direction. Are you going to let this moment pass you by? I hope you will receive the love of God that has been extended to you. St. John 3:16 says, "For God so loved the world, that he gave his only begotten Son, that whosoever believeth in him should not perish, but have everlasting life." Isn't that wonderful news? Who wouldn't serve a God like that? God loves you so much that he made a way for you when you were not even thinking about him. He is a God that is full of grace and mercy. I encourage you to come on and stop walking around with a mindset of self-hatred and receive the unconditional love of God.

God's Love Note to You:

Because he hath set his love upon me, therefore
will I deliver him: I will set him on high, because
he hath known my name.

Psalms 91:14

"Don't settle for less when you can have God's best! As you begin to call on the name of Jesus, he will show you who you really are. Personal development will begin to take place in your life. You will start seeing life in a whole new way."

Chapter 2

When I don't love myself:
I WILL SETTLE FOR LESS

Whenever you refuse to receive the love of God, you settle for less. Stop depriving yourself of this magnificent gift from God the Father. Please don't neglect this gift from Heaven above. His love looks past your faults and He is aware of your needs. Settling for less can cause you defeat in every area of your life; in your health, finances, relationships, and in your mind. I am reminded of a commercial that states "The Mind is a Terrible Thing to Waste".

Many times when we don't live our lives by walking in the love of God, we tend to fall for anything. This means there are no standards to uphold because we are living contrary to the love of God; so, for many, anything goes.

When we love God as the bible instructs us to, then He can order our steps and form us in any way He pleases. We will then not settle for anything less than God's best. We must always seek God and his kingdom first, according to St. Matthew 6:33. "But seek ye first the Kingdom of God, and his righteousness; and all these things shall be added unto you." I believe that we cannot go wrong when we put God first. I challenge you to set a special time for prayer and time alone with God. This will bring health and healing to your soul. God is looking for someone who will call upon him, just as it is stated in the book of Jeremiah 33:3, "Call unto me, and I will answer thee and shew thee great and mighty things, which thou knoweth not." Are you ready for great and mighty things? Don't settle for less when you can have God's best! As you begin to call on the name of Jesus, he will show you who you really are. Personal development will begin to take place in your life. You will start seeing life in a whole new way.

Development means to become. You must begin to allow God to work on you, so that you will not settle for less.

You want to be all that God has called you to be and to help you start in that direction; here are a few things you should know:

- ♥ Read the bible daily.

- ♥ Listen to motivational tapes and practice what you have heard.

- ♥ Listen to spiritual music that lifts your spirit and meditate on this until it gets into your spirit man.

- ♥ Purchase your Pastor's sermons on CD if they are available and review, rehearse, and remember what he has taught.

- ♥ This is really number one instead of number five…PRAY…PRAY…and PRAY!!!!

As we look back over our lives at this point, we can now truly say that God was with us all the time, even in the midst of a disobedient lifestyle.

Chapter 3

When I don't love myself:
I WILL THINK
I DON'T DESERVE THE BEST

Our past can cause us to think we don't deserve the best because in many cases, the life we lived before we accepted Christ into our lives was not a pretty one. There was a time when we practiced sin, and had no regard for God. Our lives were full of lying, cheating, stealing, backbiting, bitterness and so on, as well as all acts of disobedience. The sin nature was so strong in our lives that we did not know how to think out or bring ourselves out of what we were in. The good news is that one day, we heard the "Good News" about Jesus and he turned our lives around.

It was only Jesus that caused our spiritual eyes to be opened, so we could see that it was sin that was causing us to think that we did not deserve the best.

As we look back over our lives at this point, we can now truly say that God was with us all the time, even in the midst of a disobedient lifestyle.

God's Love Note to You:

Charity never faileth: but whether there be prophecies,
they shall fail;
whether there be tongues, they shall cease;
whether there be knowledge,
it shall vanish away.

I Corinthians 13:8

Come out with your hands up and boldly serve the Lord! Jesus took away all of our sin and shame when he shed his blood on Calvary's cross. Remember your past sins are hidden behind the cross.

Chapter 4

When I don't love myself:
I WILL HIDE BEHIND SIN AND SHAME

Too embarrassed to tell all the sinful and shameful deeds that were done unto us and that which we ourselves have done. You know that the devil would love to have it this way. However, the bible declares that we are overcomers by the blood of the lamb and by the word of our testimony. There should be a testimony of what the Lord has done in our lives. Don't let sin and shame keep you bound. St. John 8:36 tell us, "If the Son therefore shall make you free, ye shall be free indeed". Romans 8:2 remind us, "For the law of the Spirit of life in Christ Jesus hath made me free from the law of sin and death". We are free in Christ Jesus and we no longer have to hide behind the sin and shame in our lives.

Come out with your hands up and boldly serve the Lord! Jesus took away all of our sin and shame when he shed his blood on Calvary's cross. Remember your past sins are hidden behind the cross.

God's Love Note to You:

The Lord hath appeared of old unto me, saying, Yea, I

have loved thee with an everlasting love:

therefore with lovingkindness have I drawn thee.

Jeremiah 31:3

Who are you blaming? It is always so easy to

blame others for our lack of satisfaction,

but the real key to

self-happiness is learning how to take control

of our own lives and to see

the truth for what it is.

Chapter 5

WHEN I DON'T LOVE MYSELF:
I WILL PUT OTHERS TO BLAME

The word blame means accused of being at fault. The question is who are you blaming for your disappointments and discouragements? Are you blaming your mother for how you were raised and brought up in public housing with very little money? If your family had to live on government assistance, are you blaming that father who was not there while you were growing up? Do you blame your parents for the domestic violence you had to endure? The alcoholism, the drug abuse, and so many other setbacks that you feel others were to blame for your life's inconveniences. Are you blaming others because you were in a dysfunctional family? Are you blaming that child molester that touched you inappropriately or any other sexual acts committed against you?

Who are you blaming? It is always so easy to blame others for our lack of satisfaction, but the real key to self-happiness is learning how to take control of our own lives and to see the truth for what it is. The most important question we have to ask is "Am I the Problem?" Are you overlooking yourself in an effort to not focus on what the real issue is? You cannot expect someone else to fix a problem that only you can fix. Self-evaluation is the best thing that you can do for yourself. Looking within yourself and seeing who you really are is key to getting to the root of the problem. Let's start today with not blaming others for our lives. Let us take back control of our lives and trust God to show us who we are and how to love ourselves beyond life's circumstances and conditions. Let us trust God to show us who we are and to know that we are more than conquerors in Christ Jesus. Please know that I am definitely not making light of the difficult and painful experiences you may have gone through, but the truth is that God has promised to give us a peace that surpasses all of our earthly understanding. You have to allow the peace of God to get you to a place where you can move beyond the hurt, pain, guilt and shame. Let the

devil know that there will be, no more of the blame game!
I rebuke it in Jesus mighty name.

This is the day that you stop looking at others and coveting their gifts and talents and thank the Lord for what he has already placed inside of you.
You are not settling for a life of sin but striving for a life of holiness.

Chapter 6

WHEN I LOVE MYSELF:
I WON'T SETTLE FOR LESS

I t is "time out" for settling for less. God's Word declares that you are the head and not the tail; above and not beneath (Deut. 28:13). You should take on the attitude that you are not settling for less because you are fearfully and wonderfully made. (Psalms 139:14).

This is the day and the time for a shift in your thinking. No more settling for less. This is the day that you decide to seek the Lord with everything you have in you. Seek him with your whole heart, soul, and mind. He has been waiting for you to just say "Yes" to his perfect will for your life.

This is the day that you stop looking at others and coveting their gifts and talents and thank the Lord for what he has already placed inside of you. You are not settling for a life of sin but a life of holiness. I know that you have been waiting on this day to come so that you might be empowered to stand up for righteousness and declare to the Devil that YOU ARE NOT SETTLING FOR LESS!!! It is time for your prayer life to increase so that your faith can be built and be released. You must be persuaded beyond any shadow of doubt that Jesus is Lord over your life.

God's Love Note to You:

Now the end of the commandment

is charity (love) out of a pure

heart, and of a good conscience, and

of faith unfeigned:

I Timothy 1:5

The time is now; there will never be a better
time then right here and right now.
Stop being afraid of the unknown and know that
God will see you through everything
that you desire
or put your heart and mind to do.

Chapter 7

WHEN I LOVE MYSELF:
I WILL THINK I DESERVE THE BEST

Go ahead and believe in yourself. You have dreams and goals; why not see them come to pass in your life. You deserve the best because you belong to the Lord. The word "deserve" means: to be worthy. Take a few minutes and repeat to yourself "I am worthy!" When you really believe this in your heart, you will no longer allow the devil to dictate to you anymore. You will recognize that he is a liar and the father of lies. You will believe in the Lord your God and trust him alone. Now is the acceptable time that you go on and possess the land that the Lord has promised you. Do you want to write a book? Write it! Do you want to build a new home? Build it! Do you want to get in a more healthy shape? Go ahead and lose the weight!

YOU DESERVE IT BECAUSE YOU ARE WORTHY!!! Have you been dreaming of doing something great? Do it now because you deserve the best. The time is now; there will never be a better time then right here and right now. Stop being afraid of the unknown and know that God will see you through everything that you desire or put your heart and mind to do. If God gave you the dream, he will give you everything you need to see it come into fruition. You are special to him and he loves you so much. You deserve to live your best life through Jesus Christ, so go for it!

God's Love Note to You:

And we have known and believed the love

that God hath for us.

God is love; and he that dwelleth in love dwelleth in

God, and God in him.

I John 4:16

You have to open your spiritual eyes and recognize that by faith, you are in the presence of God. In God's presence, there is fullness of joy (Psalms 16:11).

Chapter 8

WHEN I LOVE MYSELF:
I WON'T HIDE BEHIND SIN AND SHAME

The bible tells us the story of Adam and Eve, who after disobeying God, were driven to hide from God, behind the sin they had committed (Genesis 3:6-8). When they were operating in disobedience, they hid themselves from the presence of God among the trees of the Garden. The word presence means: immediate surroundings. Thank God for the redemptive power through Jesus Christ because this power was the force that placed us back in the immediate presence and surrounding of God and His Glory. This means sin no longer has control of you in God's presence. Since you know this...NO MORE HIDING! No more hiding behind sin. It cannot have dominion over your life because through Jesus Christ you now live in the presence of God.

You have to open your spiritual eyes and recognize that by faith, you are in the presence of God. In God's presence, there is fullness of joy (Psalms 16:11). Therefore, instead of hiding behind sin and shame, you should be experiencing the presence of God which brings joy in the Lord in its total fullness.

God's Love Note to You:

There is no fear in love; but perfect love casteth

out fear: because fear hath torment.

He that feareth is not made perfect in love.

We love him, because he first loved us.

I John 4:18, 19

I will be like David, I will encourage myself in the Lord. I shall not die, but live and declare the works of the Lord. I know that the devil is already defeated.

Chapter 9

WHEN I LOVE MYSELF:
I WON'T PUT OTHERS TO BLAME

As you read on, open your mouth and tell the devil "No More Blaming Others!" I am taking my rightful place in the Kingdom of God. If there is anyone to blame, it will be myself. It is time that I trust totally in the Lord. I will not be discouraged easily, and if the devil sends the spirit of discouragement, it will have to flee from me. I will be like David, I will encourage myself in the Lord. I shall not die, but live and declare the works of the Lord (1 Samuel 30:6). I know that the devil is already defeated. Defeated means to win victory over. It is time that you know and live a life of victory over the devil. Amen! To God be the Glory!

Whatever God has purposed for you to do in the Kingdom, it is now time for you to come forth with the power and faith of God that he has invested in you.

Chapter 10

BECAUSE I LOVE MYSELF:
I WILL STAND STRONG AND FIGHT

Loving Yourself will cause you to stand strong and fight. No more backing down from a defeated foe (the devil). You are now able to accomplish God's purpose and plan for your life. There are no hindrances that will come to overtake your mind to cause you not to experience the love of God. In Deut. 31:6, Joshua declares to the children of Israel, to be strong and of good courage. Another thing you must do: YOU MUST FIGHT!

Fight means to struggle against a foe or enemy for a cause. Just as David questioned the men who were with him saying "What shall be done for the man who kills (fight and destroy) this Philistine and takes away the reproach from Israel? Reproach means to shame or disgrace. The devil wants to bring shame and disgrace to your life.

David went on to ask "Who is this uncircumcised Philistine that he should defy the armies of the Living God?" You are part of the army of the living God and you are to take your position and be converted and strengthen your Brethren. Whatever God has purposed for you to do in the Kingdom, it is now time for you to come forth with the power and faith of God that he has invested in you.

God's Love Note to You:

Beloved, if God loved us,

we ought also to love one another.

1 John 4:11

It is now time to continue the fight and do it with all your might. Fight for your vision, fight for your dreams! Arm yourselves with the Word of God. Fight the good fight of faith and fight for righteousness and holiness.

Chapter 11

BECAUSE I LOVE MYSELF:

I WILL FIGHT WITH ALL MY MIGHT

I know at this point you may feel that you are not qualified but don't be discouraged. You are a powerful child of God that has been through a lot of disappointments, heartache, and pain. However, through it all look at what you have gained. You have become a lot stronger, better, and wiser. These attributes were birthed out because you fought with all your might. The Lord was with you every step of the way. It is now time to continue the fight and do it with all your might. Fight for your vision, fight for your dreams! Arm yourselves with the Word of God. Fight the good fight of faith and fight for righteousness and holiness. You must be holy!

This spiritual truth comes to lead and guide you into all truth.

Paul prayed that, "The eyes of your understanding being enlightened; that ye may know what is the hope of his calling, and what the riches of the glory of his inheritance in the Saints are."

(Ephesians 1:18).

Chapter
12

BECAUSE I LOVE MYSELF:
I WILL OPEN MY EYES AND SEE

I know that you can see naturally, but it is imperative that you see spiritually. The book of Psalms 119:18 says "Open thou mine eyes, that I may behold wondrous things out of thy law". Don't you want to behold the wondrous things that Jesus has for you? His law will cause you to live a life of truth. You were bound by a lie, but now you are loosed by the spirit of truth. This spiritual truth comes to lead and guide you into all truth. Paul prayed that the eyes of your understanding be enlightened that you may know the hope of his calling, and what the riches of his inheritance in the Saints are (Ephesians 1:18).

When your eyes are opened spiritually, it will aid you to see in the spirit. You will know the hope of his calling. You will know his purpose and his assignment that you are called to complete. You must be filled with the spirit and led by the spirit. I want to touch and agree with you at this time…let's pray! Heavenly Father, we come to you just as we are. Father, I pray for your child of God, who may be reading this book. I pray that you will open their eyes so that they can see what they were not able to see before. I pray that you will fill them with your precious Holy Spirit. Father, bless their coming in and their going out. Make them the head and not the tail. Make them lenders and not borrowers. Father, cover them in the precious shed blood of your son Jesus. Help them to know the hope of your calling and give them strength to fulfill it. In Jesus name. Amen.

God's Love Note to You:

And thou shall love the Lord thy God with

all thine heart, and with all thy soul,

and with all thy might.

Deuteronomy 6:5

Now do you understand the power you possess on the inside of you? The love of God empowers you to love yourself unconditionally and with satisfaction.

You love yourself from the inside out.

Chapter 13

BECAUSE I LOVE MYSELF:
SEE THAT JESUS LIVES IN ME

Because you love yourself, you can see that Jesus lives on the inside of you. The Greater One is dwelling on the inside of you, causing you to be empowered by the Holy Spirit with an anointing that will destroy the yoke of the enemy. When you love yourself, you will realize that you now live by the Word of God. He wants you to be strengthened in your inner man. Jesus died on the cross to give you the ability to do all things through him that strengthens you. I know sometimes circumstances and situations may cause you to doubt that Jesus does live on the inside of you. People, places, and things will work to distract you from living a life of loving yourself. However, just remember that these things come to get you to stop believing the Word of God.

It will seem like a little voice is whispering in your ears, reminding you of your past mistakes and unhealthy choices. You have to remember what the Word of the Lord has declared to you. Just remember the preaching, teaching, and the prophetic words that have been spoken over your life. These things will come to test you to see if you will stand. Will you be one to hold out and watch God move in the midst of it all? I know it will be tough, but you have a much tougher God on the inside of you. You have the wisdom, knowledge, and the understanding of God in you. Don't look like you are confused or discouraged, just live according to what you have been taught.

I want to spend some time on this last verse of the poem, because it is the very thing that is going to help you make it through. I believe that it will take you to be hurt or even mistreated so that the anointing will flow out of you like never before. The anointing is an endowment of spiritual power and understanding. In the book of 1 John 2:20-27, it states, "But ye have an unction from the Holy One, and ye know all things. I have not written unto you because ye know not the truth, but because ye know it, and that no lie is of the truth. Verse 22 says, Who is a liar but he that denieth that Jesus is the Christ? He is antichrist, that denieth the Father and the Son. Whosoever denieth the Son the same hath not the Father: [but] he that acknowledgeth the Son, hath the Father also. Let that therefore abide in you, which ye have heard from the beginning. If that which ye have heard from the beginning shall remain in you, ye also shall continue in the Son, and in the Father. And this is the promise that he hath promised us, even eternal life. These things have I written unto you concerning them that seduce you. But the anointing which ye have received of him abideth in you, and ye need not that any man teach you: but as the same anointing teacheth you of all things, and is truth, and is no lie, and even as it hath taught you, ye shall abide in him."

There will be situations that will test you to see if you will abide in the truth and stand firm in the faith. You must realize and recognize that the greater one is on the inside of you. 1 John 4:4 says, "Ye are of God, little children, and have overcome them; because greater is he that is in you, than he that is in the world." 1 John 4:6 says, "We are of God: he that knoweth God heareth us; he that is not of God heareth not us. Hereby know we the spirit of truth, and the spirit of error." The Holy Spirit lives on the inside of you. 1 Corinthians 3:16 says, "Know ye not that ye are the temple of God, and that the Spirit of God dwelleth in you?" 1 Corinthians 6:19 says "What? Know ye not that your body is the temple of the Holy Ghost which is in you, which ye have of God, and you are not your own?"

Now do you understand the power you possess on the inside of you? The love of God empowers you to love yourself unconditionally and with satisfaction. You love yourself from the inside out. You are able to spread the love everywhere you go. Jesus lives in your heart and he cares for you tremendously.

As I mentioned earlier, I wanted to spend some time on this chapter of the book because it is special to me and because I feel that it is vital that we connect with these truths that have been given unto us in the Word of God.

This connection that you have with the Holy Spirit is a gift from God. Without it you will be operating from the flesh and you will not be successful at winning a spiritual war in your flesh. You must not forget that this is a spiritual battle that you are in, Ephesians 6:12.

I am making this very personal because as I talk with you, I am hearing the Holy Spirit talking to me first. Again, as I am hearing the voice of the Lord, I must remember that I must be a partaker of the revelation of Jesus Christ first before I can empower others to do the same. My sincere prayer is that you love yourself with the love of God and never let anything bring doubt to your mind that would cause you to think otherwise. Always remember to never settle for less, because you deserve the best.

About the Author

Renee' Hall is a born again believer. God called and saved her in 1995. Over the past 17 years God has poured His love on her and has taught her by the Holy Spirit how to love herself. Renee' went through most of her life not understanding how to love herself as God loves. As she grew spiritually, with much prayer, reading the Word of God, and fasting, she learned how to truly love herself with the unconditional love of God. Renee''s mandate is to spread this love and teach others to truly love themselves through the agape love of God.

Contact the Author

Please contact the author with any comments you may have. You are also welcome to contact her for bookings. As the Holy Spirit leads, Renee' is available for book club presentations, signings, or speaking engagements for your church or organization (women's ministries, conferences, workshops, retreats, and seminars).

Contact Renee' Hall at:
lovingmyselfent@ymail.com
352-359-7758

More From Renee' Hall

Renee' is currently working on, and anticipating her second book. She has created a perfume line called *Loving Myself.* Renee' recently release Vol. 1 perfume in her fragrance line called "Dream". Renee''s vision also includes fashion. She has created t-shirts with the *Loving Myself* poem on them. The t-shirts are sure to make a fashion statement, and are available in the colors of white or pink.

Renee' is presently working on an inspirational *Loving Myself* CD which is anticipated to be released in the Fall of 2012.

Renee' is also affiliated with the Women at the Well Tour (Visionary Sabriena Williams). This empowerment tour features eight women of God traveling together from city to city preaching and teaching the Word of God.

Renee' has a vision for Loving Myself Enterprises, which she prays will continue to be a blessing to the Kingdom of God.

www.ingramcontent.com/pod-product-compliance
Lightning Source LLC
Chambersburg PA
CBHW060041040426
42331CB00032B/1990

About The Author

Donald Grant is a husband, cook, cat lover, high handicap golfer, and poet. Usually in that order. Living on the Central Coast of California, most days include a walk along the beach with his wife. Raised as a military brat, he has lived in various parts of the United States and spent several years in North Africa. During his life he has been an engineer, a minister, and small business owner. He loves to comment on life and when something attracts his attention, he will add his thoughts to a poem or two.

www.ingramcontent.com/pod-product-compliance
Lightning Source LLC
Chambersburg PA
CBHW071926020426
42331CB00010B/2748